# FCE

## PRACTICE TESTS **1**

## Teacher's book

**Virginia Evans**

**Jenny Dooley**

**Express Publishing**

Published by *Express Publishing*

Liberty House, New Greenham Park, Newbury, Berkshire RG19 6HW
Tel: (0044) -1635 817 363 - Fax: (0044) -1635 817 463
e-mail:inquiries@expresspublishing.co.uk
INTERNET http: //www.expresspublishing.co.uk

©    *Virginia Evans - Jenny Dooley, 1996*

First published 1996
New Edition 2000

ISBN 1-84216-806-1

# Contents

# Test 1

## Paper 1 - Reading

**Part 1**  1. D   2. A   3. H   4. G   5. I   6. E   7. B

**Part 2**
8. D (Ln 1-2)    12. B (Ln 23)
9. A (Ln 5-6)    13. C (Ln 33-34)
10. C (Ln 13-14)  14. B (Ln 38)
11. D (Ln 20-21)  15. C (Ln 39-40)

**Part 3**  16. A  17. H  18. B  19. F  20. C  21. G

**Part 4**
22/23. B, F in any order    31. B
24. C                        32. C
25/26. F, G in any order     33. D
27/28. B, E in any order     34. E
29/30. B, D in any order     35. B

## Paper 2 - Writing

### Part 1

Dear Mr Dixon,

 I am writing in response to your advertisement for activity holidays and would be grateful if you would provide me with the following information.

 First of all, I would like to know if there are any restrictions for the children? My younger child is twelve, the other is fourteen. Both are very interested in arts and crafts.

 Neither of them can swim yet and need to learn so I would like to know whether the swimming instructors are fully qualified. If they wish to participate in photography do they need to bring their own cameras, or is equipment provided? I'd also like to know where the centre is situated - is it near the town centre, or in the countryside? I realise that I'm rather late in booking and I wonder if there are any places left for the last two weeks in August. If so, how much is the deposit, and when would you require it?

 Thank you very much for your help.

Yours sincerely

### Part 2

**2. Suggested points to cover:**
- **Introduction:** reason for survey, details of children surveyed (eg. sex, age, social and educational background, interests etc)
- **Details:** of findings - (under different headings) traditional toys, computer games etc
- **Conclusion:** Suggest reasons for your findings. e.g. Boys were found to prefer computer games more than girls.

**3. Suggested points to cover:**
- Thank pen friend for letter
- Explain about traditional music
- Describe some of the dances that accompany the music and what they mean
- Describe popular music eg rock etc
- Briefly explain which you prefer and why
- Offer to send a cassette
- Wish friend well with their project

## Paper 3 - Use of English

**Part 1**
1. C   4. C   7. B   10. A   13. B
2. A   5. A   8. D   11. C   14. C
3. D   6. B   9. C   12. D   15. A

**Part 2**
16. used/accustomed    24. which
17. come               25. that
18. from/with          26. into
19. full               27. known
20. least              28. due
21. make/find          29. so
22. that               30. up/apart
23. have/need

**Part 3**
31. ... has been ruined by ...
32. ... 'd/would rather not tell ...
33. ... look after the dog ...
34. ... not approve of my/me staying ...
35. ... might not come ...
36. ... made all of us go ...
37. ... Tim had not overslept ...
38. ... have to be taken on ...
39. ... is said to have been ...
40. ... with a view to buying ...

**Part 4**
41. ✓        45. ✓        49. it    53. on
42. been     46. for      50. ✓     54. to
43. a        47. one      51. such  55. ✓
44. the      48. itself   52. ✓

**Part 5**
56. majority       61. particularly
57. choice         62. communication
58. knowledge      63. decision
59. possibility    64. temporarily
60. advancement    65. pleasure

## Listening Test 1

**Part 1**   1. C    3. C    5. B    7. B
             2. B    4. B    6. A    8. C

**Part 2**   9. 4 pm Tuesday
             10. five years
             11. organising sport
             12. Jane
             13. outside the school building
             14. £6.50 per week
             15. lose your deposit
             16. cycle/ride their bikes
             17. on Sundays
             18. show/have their passport

**Part 3**   19. D   20. A   21. E   22. C   23. F

**Part 4**   24. T   26. F   28. T   30. F
             25. F   27. F   29. F

### Tapescript (Listening Test 1)

### Part 1

*You'll hear people talking in eight different situations. For questions 1 to 8, choose the best answer, A, B or C.*

**1.** *You'll hear a man talking to a receptionist. Who does he want to speak to ?*
   A   *Mr Grey*
   B   *Mr Sands*
   C   *Mr Gail*

**Receptionist:** Hello, Mr Grey how can I help you?
**Man:** I'd like to speak to the Manager, please.
**Receptionist:** Is that Mr Gail, Manager of Services, or the Manager of Information, Mr Sands?
**Man:** Ummm, I need to talk about the new road plans.
**Receptionist:** I'll just call Services then.

**2.** *You will hear a man complaining at the opera. Why is he complaining?*
   A   *The tickets were too expensive.*
   B   *He didn't get the seats he wanted.*
   C   *He wanted seats in the circle.*

**Man:** You just don't understand, do you? I'm not leaving until I get my money back. You promised me the best seats in the house and what did we get when we arrived? Stuck on the side of the circle with a pillar blocking our view. *And* I paid £50 for the privilege.

**3.** *Listen to a woman describing her hotel to a friend. What was wrong with the hotel?*
   A   *It wasn't near the beach.*
   B   *It had a dirty swimming pool.*
   C   *It had no swimming pool.*

**Woman:** We had a look around the hotel as soon as we got there. It was great... near the sea, really nice. But I suddenly wondered - where's the swimming pool? We wandered around looking for it, then behind all this rubbish, trees and plants we found it. Well, we thought we had but it was actually a pond with fish and ducks in it.

**4.** *Listen to this announcement. What time will the flight leave?*
   A   *6.45*
   B   *8.45*
   C   *9.45*

**Announcement:** This is an announcement for all passengers booked on flight EF704 to Geneva. Due to a technical problem the flight has been delayed and will not take off at the expected time of 6.45 pm. There will be a delay of one and a half hours before boarding. Take-off is expected half an hour after that. We apologise for this delay.

**5.** *You overhear this conversation. Why is Mary late for work?*
   A   *There was heavy traffic on the roads.*
   B   *Her alarm clock didn't go off.*
   C   *She had had a late night.*

**Mary:** Good morning, Mr Rodgers.
**Mr Rodgers:** Late again Mary? What was it this time? Heavy traffic? Late night? This really isn't good enough.
**Mary:** Well, actually, there *was* heavy traffic, but the batteries in my alarm clock had run out. I suppose I should have noticed, but I was really tired when I went to bed.
**Mr Rodgers:** Well, just don't let it happen again.

**6.** *Listen to this conversation between Rachel and her teacher. Why has Rachel not done her homework?*
   A   *She didn't understand it.*
   B   *She was too busy.*
   C   *She didn't want to do it.*

**Mr Hurst:** Rachel, where's your homework?
**Rachel:** Er, I haven't done it, sir.
**Mr Hurst:** You didn't have time, is that it?
**Rachel:** No, sir ... I ...
**Mr Hurst:** (sarcastic) Oh, I see... so you just couldn't be bothered then! I suppose you had something far better to do, did you, like watching TV or... or... going shopping with your friends or something!
**Rachel:** (upset) No! That's not it. I just didn't know exactly what I had to do!
**Mr Hurst:** (mollified) Aah... I see... well that's different then ...

**7.** *George is at the pub talking to a friend about his new job. Why is he so disappointed?*
   A   *He doesn't like the people he works with.*
   B   *He wants more responsibility.*
   C   *The job doesn't pay very well.*

*George:* Don't get me wrong, I do enjoy the job and everything ... it's just when I had the interview I thought I'd be running the finance department you know and er...

*Dave:* Well anyway, what about your colleagues?

*George:* Oh... very cold at first, but I've made friends with one or two of them now.

*Dave:* And what's the money like?

*George:* I can't complain about that Dave. I just wish I was in charge of things, like I was in my old job.

*Dave:* Give it time, give it time...

8. *Mrs Jones is talking to her doctor. Why doesn't he want to prescribe any medicine for her?*

   A  *It would be dangerous.*
   B  *He doesn't know what's wrong with her.*
   C  *It isn't necessary.*

   *Mrs Jones:* Cough ... cough. You see doctor, I've got this awful cough.

   *Doctor:* Hmm... Well your chest doesn't sound too bad. Do you have a temperature?

   *Mrs Jones:* Well, I'm a bit hot but no... not really.

   *Doctor:* You've just got a bit of a cold...

   *Mrs Jones:* I really would like something for it, please doctor.

   *Doctor:* Look, I could give you some medicine but I don't see the point.

   *Mrs Jones:* Do you think it would be bad for me, doctor?

   *Doctor:* No, it probably wouldn't. I just don't want to give you something you simply do not need.

   *Mrs Jones:* (disappointed) Oh... oh I see...

## Part 2

*You'll hear the Information Manager of a language school giving a talk to a new group of foreign students. For questions 9 to 18, complete the notes which summarise what the speaker says. You will need to write a word or short phrase in each box.*

Welcome everybody to The Anglo Academy of English. We hope your stay here is a pleasant one. I'm going to hand out an information pack to you which tells you about things to do while you're here. It contains a questionnaire which I'd like you to fill in and give back to us by 4 pm on Tuesday.

Just in case you don't know, my name is Claire and, I'm the Information Officer for the school. Though I've only been at AAE for about 5 years I lived in Sussex for over 10 years so I'm sure you'll agree with me when I say I know the place really well. My job is to organise everything you do outside class time, and to help me I have two assistants, Ben and Jane. Ben, on my right here, is in charge of organising things like volleyball, football, hockey and swimming. And Jane, here on my left, is the person you need to see if you are unhappy about your accommodation.

I'll be coming around the classrooms to talk to groups individually, but I'd just like to make a few announcements while you're all here together. Please remember that there is to be no smoking anywhere inside the building at any time. Anyone wishing to hire a bicycle can do so from Mr Grey who will be here at lunch-time. Bicycles cost £8.00 per week for anyone over 16 and £6.50 a week if you are under 16. A deposit of £20.00 is required and will be returned to you at the end of your stay as long as your bicycle hasn't been damaged. Please note that for your own safety there is to be no cycling along this road, which is the busiest in the town. Please also remember that in England we drive on the left!

My office is along the corridor on the right and I am there every day from 10 am to 6 pm except Sundays. I'll be there in about 20 minutes if anyone wants me to issue them with an identity card for students. Fortunately you won't need a photograph, just your passport.

I'll now hand you over to Vicky, the Director of Studies, who will tell you a little about your course here. Once again I'd like to wish you a very enjoyable stay.

## Part 3

*You'll hear five people talking about objects they use for carrying things. For questions 19 to 23, choose from the list of objects A to F what each speaker is describing. Use the letters only once. There is one extra letter which you do not need to use.*

*Speaker 1 (female):* I only take this out about once a year - it's usually stored in the loft the rest of the year. I bought it when I organised a trip around Southeast Asia for myself and two friends and it was so handy being able to put so many things in and being able to find them so quickly. Mine has little pockets all over the place - I can put all sorts of things in it; first-aid kit, camping stove, penknife, toilet roll and many other things. And it's so easy to carry - you just put it on your back - tie the straps and off you go. You can walk for ages with something like 20kg on your back.

*Speaker 2 (female):* Mine's truly wonderful. I was given it as a Christmas present and, to be honest, I was quite disappointed when the handle on my other one broke and I had to pull this one out of the cupboard. But now I think it's great - even though it's quite small I can carry lots of things in it - money, a bit of make-up, some personal papers and my credit cards. It's even got a little compartment that closes with a zip - I keep all my little secrets in there, you know.

*Speaker 3 (female):* I know it's a bit ugly, but it's very spacious and practical. It's made of canvas or something; I don't think you can get them in leather - and anyway I can't imagine a housewife paying lots of money to get a leather one. I usually carry it with me all the time, just in case I need to pop into the shop to get something - I don't believe in wasting things - so I usually refuse to take any of those bags at the check out. Anyway, you'd be surprised at exactly how much I can get in there and how strong it is.

*Speaker 4 (male):* Last weekend my wife and I were getting ready to go away, and my wife just laughed when I got it out. She claimed that we'd had it for so long that it looked like an antique. But I can't part with it - we've had it for so many years and have been on so many trips with it. It's got stickers from lots of countries on it. Admittedly it's not as good as some of those new ones that have wheels and a handle to pull them along, but the material's really strong on ours - I think it's made of leather or something similar. Anyway we manage to fit everything we need in it when we go away.

*Speaker 5 (male):* I've got a hard one. You get so much more wear out of them than you do out of soft ones. I used to have a soft one, but I always found that things got wet when it rained. But this one's waterproof and my documents never get ruined. There's also enough space in it for my personal belongings too - er ... I've got a ... er ... comb, my credit cards and cheque books, personal organiser and even my mobile phone....

## Part 4

*You'll hear a conversation which takes place in a house between two old friends, Cathy Murray and Bridget Allan, who have not seen each other for a while. Answer questions 24 to 30 by writing T (for true) or F (for false) in the boxes provided.*

*Bridget:* Oh, hello Cathy. It's you! Come in, come in. Come through and have a seat.

*Cathy:* Hello Bridget. I was just shopping nearby so I thought I'd drop in.

*Bridget:* Well it's been a long time. I haven't seen you since the St Patrick's night dance at the club.

*Cathy:* Has it been that long?

*Bridget:* It has, Cathy, it has. Can I get you a drink? The tea's just brewing.

*Cathy:* A cup of tea would be nice. I've been on my feet all day, trying to get everything sorted out for our Joseph's wedding.

*Bridget:* Did I hear you say wedding, Cathy? Lovely! Who's the lucky girl?

*Cathy:* It's a girl he was at university with. She's a primary school teacher, a really quiet person. A grand girl.

*Bridget:* When's the big day?

*Cathy:* Oh, it's not for a few weeks yet, but there's so much to do and everything's so expensive.

*Bridget:* Tell me about it. I'm sure that every time I go to the supermarket the prices have gone up. Daylight robbery, that's what it is.

*Cathy:* Have you heard that Mackays, the newspaper shop, is closing down?

*Bridget:* That's the third shop that's closed down in as many weeks, you know Cathy. And they say there's an economic recovery. These politicians, they don't know what they're talking about.

*Cathy:* I know. But it's the young people I feel sorry for. It's not as if they don't **want** to work.

*Bridget:* True. That's why my nephew James is leaving. There's nothing for him here. Four years at university and what happens? He's been unemployed for 2 years, applied for hundreds of jobs, so he's decided he's had enough. He's going to Australia.

*Cathy:* Is he? Good for him. Bernie and Dot won't be too happy though. He's their only child.

*Bridget:* True, but what do they expect? At least in Australia he'll have the chance of a real job. Though it'll be difficult because Dot's been sick.

*Cathy:* Yes, I saw her last week and she was quite bad.

*Bridget:* Yes, it's been really hard for Bernie.

*Cathy:* Let's hope she gets better soon, because Bernie had to give up his job to look after her. How's Bill by the way?

*Bridget:* He's OK, I guess. He's still working, but he's been ill lately. He's tired all the time but he won't take any time off work. I just wish he'd retire then we could go and live in Lanzarote. Remember we've been going to the same villa for over 20 years. It's like a second home to us now.

*Cathy:* I'd miss you though, Bridget. We've been through a lot together. But life goes on, eh? Life goes on.

*Bridget:* You're not going to get all sentimental on me now Cathy, are you? Now when am I going to get that wedding invitation?

## Speaking Test 1

### Part 2 (Suggested answers)

### Pictures A and B

- In **picture A** a group of elderly people are playing a board game together. In **picture B** a group of young people dressed in ski clothes are sitting in the snow and posing for the camera, while somebody in the background is skiing. The young people are very active, whereas the old people are not.

- Residents of old people's homes spend a lot of their time watching television and talking to the other residents. Some people like to paint or draw pictures, while others like to write letters to their relatives or friends.

- When you are young you can do anything you want, whereas when you are older you are restricted to doing those things which are not active.

- I spend my free time playing basketball or volleyball with my friends. I also like going down to the amusement arcade to play on the electronic computer games. I'm also building up a large stamp collection.

## Pictures C and D

- I think the lifestyles of the two people in the pictures must be greatly affected by the climate they have to live in. The boy in **picture C** is an Eskimo (Inuit) and so he would have to dress warmly. Ice and snow must be the biggest problems that he has to deal with daily. The woman in **picture D** probably lives in Africa where it is very hot. As there is not a lot of water there, she would have to think carefully about how she uses it.

- The Eskimo (Inuit) boy probably spends his time fishing and building igloos by cutting blocks of ice. The woman in picture D lives in Africa, and I think she probably spends a lot of her time carrying water and preparing food for her family. She also needs to look after her animals.

- I am fascinated by the Chinese, as their culture is so different to ours. They speak a language that is very different to ours. They eat a lot of rice and noodles out of small bowls with chopsticks.

- Some cultures are dying out as their countries are inhabited or invaded by foreigners. Many countries have been "Americanised", so that the native people no longer eat their own national food, or listen to ethnic music but that which is bought from America.

## Part 3

- **SA:** One picture shows a rainforest on fire. Although I think this is a serious environmental problem, I don't think the destruction of the rainforests will cause the end of the world.

- **SB:** I agree, and I think that nuclear power stations do pose a real threat to the world.

- **SA:** Yes. Look what happened at Chernobyl. If nuclear power is used carelessly then some serious problems could arise.

- **SB:** The picture of a man trapped inside a computer shows how man is becoming a slave to computers. I do think that computers could be a problem in the future because we rely on them so heavily, but I don't think they could cause global destruction.

- **SA:** But don't forget that many countries' defence mechanisms are linked up to a computer system. One problem with the computer could lead to the launching of a nuclear bomb which would cause an explosion, as in the picture.

- **SB:** Yes, a nuclear war would definitely cause global destruction. Whereas I don't think conventional warfare (warfare without nuclear weapons) would be responsible for the end of the world.

## Part 4

- **SA:** One of the biggest problems that the world faces today is environmental. The hole in the ozone layer is growing, and if people don't stop polluting the atmosphere the effects will be irreversible.

- **SB:** I agree that the environment is a serious issue, but what worries me are the wars. There are always countries at war, but at least most of them haven't got any nuclear weapons.

- **SA:** There should be a world ban on anything that causes pollution. Packaging for all products should be biodegradable, and factories should be made to decrease their pollution output, and rainforests should be replanted.

- **SB:** As for nuclear weapons, I think that they should all be confiscated and destroyed.

- **SA:** The problem with nuclear weapons is that once you've invented something you can't "uninvent" it! It exists now and so the problem has to be dealt with.

- **SA:** All people should be taught from an early age what is right and wrong. If there wasn't so much violence on television, then maybe people wouldn't be so violent towards each other.

- **SB:** I think more attention should be given to organisations such as the U.N. which try and maintain peace in the world.

- **SA:** I think it is ultimately up to individuals to look after the world. Every person can do a lot to protect the world we live in.

- **SB:** I don't agree. I think individuals are powerless and the governments hold all the power. Therefore I think it is the governments' responsibility to try and make the world a cleaner, safer and better place to live.

# Test 2

## Paper 1 - Reading

**Part 1**   1. G   2. A   3. D   4. H   5. F   6. B

**Part 2**
7. C (Ln 5-6)
8. D (Ln 8-10)
9. C (Ln 12-14)
10. A (Ln 22-24)
11. B (Ln 27-29)
12. C (Ln 33-38)
13. D (Ln 41)

**Part 3**
14. B   16. I   18. H   20. G
15. D   17. A   19. E

**Part 4**
21. C
22. C
23. A
24. C
25. E
26/27. A, D
(in any order)
28. D
29. C
30. B
31. C
32. B
33. A
34. E
35. B

## Paper 2 - Writing

### Part 1

Dear Mr Ericson,
  Thank you very much for your offer of sharing your knowledge with me.
  I'd very much like to interview you. I wonder if Saturday June 17th at 4 pm would suit you? I will come to your house as I imagine that would be easier, particularly if there is anything you wish to show me; old photographs of your family or of the town, for example. If so, I'd be delighted to see them, and any old newspapers or magazines you might have. I'd also like to know if you have kept in touch with any old school friends, as I would like to interview as many people as possible. I'm also interested in family trees and would love to hear about yours. And, if you don't mind, I'd like to take your photograph.
  I look forward to meeting you.

Your sincerely,
Dwayne Pipe

### Part 2

**Start letter** - Dear X... How are you etc.
- Explain that sister is getting married and invite friend
- Details of wedding - the bride's dress
  - the garlands
  - best man and woman
  - rice throwing
  - bombonieres
  - the party and dancing
- Repeat the invitation
- Sign off

## Part 3

**State topic**
- arguments for - eg students will be more interested and learn more if they can study what they want
- arguments against - eg students may miss out important subjects and won't get a good all round education
- conclusion - eg improved choice may help to motivate students and be beneficial as long as the core subjects eg English, Maths, Science and a language are compulsory.

## Paper 3 - Use of English

**Part 1**
1. A   4. D   7. A   10. C   13. D
2. C   5. A   8. D   11. A   14. B
3. C   6. C   9. D   12. C   15. A

**Part 2**
16. more
17. time
18. ago
19. would
20. take
21. like
22. other
23. reached
24. with
25. being
26. ones
27. paying
28. form
29. make
30. ways/means/methods

**Part 3**
31. ... on no account will he ...
32. ... in case I want to ...
33. ... he would not have ...
34. ... had my TV stolen ...
35. ... need not have run ...
36. ... was such a difficult exam ...
37. ... ruined his name/gave him a bad name ...
38. ... are going to be interviewed ...
39. ... would rather you did not ...
40. ... is her intention to work ...

**Part 4**
41. we
42. be
43. at
44. ✓
45. its
46. ✓
47. it
48. in
49. had
50. ✓
51. he
52. who
53. ✓
54. seeing
55. up

**Part 5**
56. comfortable
57. relatively
58. belongings
59. storage
60. regulations
61. sensitive
62. detectors
63. securely
64. enjoyment
65. entertaining

## Listening Test 2

**Part 1**
| | | | | | | | |
|---|---|---|---|---|---|---|---|
| 1. | B | 3. | A | 5. | B | 7. | C |
| 2. | B | 4. | A | 6. | B | 8. | A |

**Part 2**
9. not known/given
10. 10 minutes
11. 20-25 minutes
12. delicious
13. £10.75
14. quite good
15. not good/dissatisfied/not impressed/ not pleased
16. (very) pleasant
17. (very) wide
18. bad service/service not very good

**Part 3**  19. E  20. C  21. F  22. B  23. D

**Part 4**
| | | | | | | | |
|---|---|---|---|---|---|---|---|
| 24. | C | 26. | C | 28. | C | 30. | B |
| 25. | B | 27. | B | 29. | A | | |

## Tapescript (Listening Test 2)

### Part 1

*You'll hear people talking in eight different situations. For questions 1 to 8, choose the best answer, A, B or C.*

1. *You hear this man talking about his job. Who does he work for?*
   A  his friends
   B  himself
   C  a hospital

   **Man:** Well, er, I used to do it for friends you know, it was word of mouth basically. People knew I needed the money because I'd lost my job and then been in hospital for ages, so if they needed a bit of decorating or whatever done, they'd call me. I've given all that up now of course, because after a while I started getting contracts from companies. I can charge more, the jobs are bigger, and I can choose when I take my holidays. It's much better...

2. *You hear this woman describing a party. What was it for?*
   A  a family reunion
   B  her parents' wedding anniversary
   C  her own wedding anniversary

   **Woman:** It was a fantastic surprise. They really didn't suspect a thing. All of us were there except my brother Dan, who's in Australia and couldn't come back. But my sister was there. They've been married for forty years you know and it's just nice to celebrate these things. You should've seen their faces when they opened the door and saw...

3. *You overhear a man talking. Where is he?*
   A  at a bus stop
   B  at a train station
   C  in a taxi queue

   **Man:** ...(breathless)...Excuse me, have you been waiting long? I'm in a real hurry and I'm wondering if I should go and get a taxi instead, because I can't spend all day here waiting for a number three - it's a really unreliable service, isn't it? I'd get the train if there was a station nearby, but unfortunately it's miles away...(fade)

4. *Listen to two film critics discussing a new film. What is the woman's opinion of the film?*
   A  She liked it.
   B  She preferred the director's previous films.
   C  She has no particular opinion.

   **Man:** I much preferred his earlier films. They were so much better made, the scripts were sharper...
   **Woman:** I disagree entirely. I thought his first few films were, well, nothing special, but this was way ahead of anything else he's done.
   **Man:** Well, I found it dull. Yes, that's it frankly.
   **Woman:** I'm afraid I simply don't agree.

5. *Listen to this woman talking in a shop. Why does she want to buy an electric cooker?*
   A  It is cheaper.
   B  It is safer.
   C  It looks better.

   **Woman:** Excuse me, um ... I'm looking for a new cooker.
   **Salesman:** Certainly, madam. This one is very good value.
   **Woman:** I'm not sure I want gas though. I mean, isn't it rather dangerous?
   **Salesman:** Well, not really - not nowadays. And the electric ones cost a lot more, madam.
   **Woman:** That doesn't matter. I do like the look of the gas one, but I'll take the other one - you can't be too careful, especially when you've got young children.

6. *You will hear a woman talking about a frightening experience. Why was she frightened?*
   A  Someone attacked her.
   B  Someone was following her.
   C  She was on her own.

   **Woman:** I was walking home from Meg's at about 11 o'clock, so it was dark, but that was okay, and I'm used to going all over the place on my own. But then I heard these footsteps behind me getting closer and closer. I was really scared and beginning to panic, when suddenly there was a tap on my shoulder. I screamed and turned around, but it was only Meg's brother. I'd left my keys at their flat and he wanted to give them back. I felt like such a fool...

11

**7.** *You will hear part of a council meeting on how a government grant is to be used. What does the council intend to do?*
   A *build a new leisure centre*
   B *build a new school*
   C *buy new school equipment*

**Councillor:** We debated at length about this. Originally, we wanted to spend the money on a new swimming pool, gym, or a sort of health and sports complex. This was a popular plan, but educational needs must be a priority. Our schools have been under-financed for years. We'd like to build a new school, but the grant just isn't big enough, so we intend to provide all the local schools with new books, televisions and videos for all classrooms, better sporting facilities...(fade)

**8.** *You hear two flatmates talking. Why won't Dave let Bill borrow his boots?*
   A *They're the wrong size.*
   B *There's a hole in them.*
   C *They're his only pair.*

**Bill:** Dave, can I borrow your boots?
**Dave:** Which ones?
**Bill:** The brown leather ones. You know - you've just had the hole fixed.
**Dave:** Oh yeah. Well, no, I'd rather you didn't Bill.
**Bill:** Why not? You don't need them, you've got loads of different ones.
**Dave:** It's not that, but last time I lent you my shoes, you stretched them. Your feet are bigger than mine.

## Part 2

*You'll hear a woman being interviewed about a restaurant. For questions 9 to 18, complete the notes which summarise what the speakers say.*

**Interviewer:** Excuse me sir and madam, do you mind if I ask you a few questions? Foraglio's Pizza are conducting a survey to see if our customers are satisfied.
**Woman:** Oh, I see...er, well, go ahead.
**Interviewer:** You're not in a hurry, are you?
**Woman:** No, we were just going home.
**Interviewer:** Okay, good. Er, it's just *your* answers I require, madam, not your husband's.
**Woman:** Oh, Okay.
**Interviewer:** Good. First of all, can you remember your waitress' name?
**Woman:** Um, I don't know to be honest. I don't think she told us.
**Interviewer:** Oh? Well, she should have.
**Woman:** No, no I definitely don't know.
**Interviewer:** That's a shame. Anyway, how long was it before the unnamed waitress (laughs) took your order.
**Woman:** I'm not sure, but I don't think it was very long - about 5 minutes, no, nearer ten I'd say.

**Interviewer:** Okay. And did you have to wait long for your meal once you'd ordered?
**Woman:** Good question...we were so busy talking. But I know it was quite a long time because I remember looking up and seeing other people getting their food before us...it must have been about 20 to 25 minutes.
**Interviewer:** Okay, thanks. So, when the food finally arrived, what did you think of it?
**Woman:** To be honest, my husband didn't enjoy his spaghetti at all. It was lukewarm and too salty. But my pizza was delicious.
**Interviewer:** Okay. It's only *your* answers we require madam, as I said.
**Woman:** Yes, right.
**Interviewer:** So, was it worth it? Oh yes, and how much did you pay, by the way?
**Woman:** Just for my meal? Well, I'll let you work it out. Between us we paid £21.50 for two meals that cost the same.
**Interviewer:** I see you're making me work for my money! So that makes, er, 10 pounds and er 25...no, 75 pence.
**Woman:** And to answer your other question, that price, hmm, I'd say we got our money's worth.
**Interviewer:** And what about the general standard of cleanliness in the restaurant?
**Woman:** Well our tablecloth was dirty and I had to ask for a clean glass as well.
**Interviewer:** Oh dear. So you weren't impressed.
**Woman:** No. No, we weren't really very pleased.
**Interviewer:** Not many questions left. Thanks for being so patient.
**Woman:** No problem.
**Interviewer:** Okay. Where were we? Oh yes...how did you find the surroundings - the furniture, fittings, lighting, music and so on?
**Woman:** The lighting was nice and soft. And the music, well in some places it's far too loud - I mean, you can hardly hear yourself talk - but here it was perfect. Not too loud. Overall, I thought it was very pleasant.
**Interviewer:** Good...now on to the menu. Did it offer a wide variety?
**Woman:** There definitely was plenty of choice...I hadn't heard of half the things actually!
**Interviewer:** Right...okay...now before we finish would you like to add anything?
**Woman:** Er...well I didn't think much of the service to be honest - we waited for ages.
**Interviewer:** Okay, fair enough. I do hope that doesn't mean you won't be coming back?
**Woman:** No, no...I expect we'll give the place another try.
**Interviewer:** I hope you do. Thanks very much for your help. Goodbye.
**Woman:** My pleasure. Bye.

## Part 3

*You'll hear five people talking about what happened on the way to work. For questions 19 to 23 choose from the list A to F which statement applies to each speaker. Use the letters only once. There is one extra letter which you do not need to use.*

**Speaker 1 (Male):** Well I got up in plenty of time and I left the house at eight as usual, didn't think there'd be a problem, but then I noticed there didn't seem to be any buses around, and the traffic was heavier than usual. Then I caught sight of a headline in the paper saying that the buses had gone on strike. So in the end, I got a taxi and didn't get in till nine forty-five - the boss went mad!

**Speaker 2 (Male):** It was last Wednesday. I thought I was going to miss the bus because when I looked at my watch I realised I was a bit late. But I ran for it and got it and I thought, "Phew, thank goodness!" Then there was this almighty crash; the bus had collided with a lorry, and a couple of pedestrians were hurt. Of course, we all had to get off the bus and wait for the next one, but luckily it came straightaway so I got to the office just a few minutes late.

**Speaker 3 (Male):** I don't know how it happened because it's a new one, I only bought it the other day. Anyway, I was walking down the road, and I couldn't understand what was going on because it was only a quarter past eight, yet there were loads more people around than usual at that time. There was I, calmly walking along thinking I had plenty of time, when I looked at the station clock and realised it was actually ten to nine - my watch must've stopped. I didn't get in till 9.30 and I'm supposed to start at 9.

**Speaker 4 (Female):** When I woke up it was a beautiful day, so I put on something summery and set off for work. It was such lovely weather I went through the park. Then I realised I'd forgotten to put on my watch. I can't manage without it, so I had to run back to the house for it. I thought I'd be late as I saw my bus leaving, but then another one came immediately so that was okay and I wasn't too late.

**Speaker 5 (Female):** I hadn't been late once this year. I used to be late all the time, do you remember? Anyway, I left the house and tried to start the car but for some reason it wouldn't start. I was running late by then, but I remembered that there was a bus at 8.30 which would get me to work on time. But when I got to the bus station I couldn't remember which number bus I needed. By the time I asked an inspector, the bus had just left so I got to work over an hour later than I should have done.

## Part 4

*You'll hear a man being interviewed about a round-the-world expedition. For questions 24 to 30, decide which of the choices A, B or C is the correct answer.*

**Interviewer:** Today in the studio we are talking to Ralph Findlayson, the explorer who last week completed a round-the-world expedition via the North and South Poles. Welcome Ralph.

**Ralph:** Thank you.

**Interviewer:** What a fantastic achievement. You must be very proud.

**Ralph:** (reticent) Well...er...yes...

**Interviewer:** And it took a lot of determination. I believe it took several years for the idea to become reality.

**Ralph:** Yes...er, my wife Victoria originally suggested it in er...1985. We sought the advice of the world famous explorer, Sir Gregory Narchon, who was very, very helpful...anyway, for various reasons, we did not actually leave Britain until 1992. I would never have thought it would take so long to organise everything.

**Interviewer:** Indeed. Why exactly *did* it take so long?

**Ralph:** Well, we managed to get sponsorship from several major companies almost immediately, so funding wasn't a problem. And although it took some time, with very careful interviewing we managed to find some marvellous people to form our crew. The real problem was bureaucracy. Obviously, they can't let just anyone go to the Polar ice caps...we had to prove that we were serious about the trip, that we knew what we were doing, and in the end it took several years to get the green light.

**Interviewer:** You mentioned your wife Victoria.

**Ralph:** Yes.

**Interviewer:** She must be quite an amazing person. I believe she is something of a feminist - is this what motivated her to come with you?

**Ralph:** Hardly! Vicky doesn't hold with all that - she thinks, as I do, that men and women are different and have different things to offer. Having said that, she is a skilled radio operator. But no, no the real reason was that the expedition was going to last for 3 years and neither of us wanted to be apart for such a long period of time.

**Interviewer:** I see. Now is it true that you had some terrible fights with the other members of the team, Ben and Simon, out there in the Antarctic?

**Ralph:** Well, ... in fact, ... for the most part we got on extremely well. They respected me as the leader of the expedition and trusted my knowledge and decisions. But sometimes, because we were sharing a small tent and were very stressed and anxious, we did quarrel as anybody would. But very little really.

**Interviewer:** How did you actually cross both polar ice caps? With dogs and sledges?

**Ralph:** Well, originally that was what we were going to do, as several other explorers had told us that dog-pulled sledges were best, but in the end we used skidoos - sledges operated by battery, because we'd also heard that dogs often don't survive the journey to the ice caps. I intend to do my next polar expedition on foot though.

**Interviewer:** Really? That will be a challenge! One final question, Ralph. I've read your book and found it very interesting. But as I read of the hardship and suffering you went through on the expedition, I couldn't help but wonder why on earth you did it.

**Ralph:** A good question. Perhaps I could've stayed in England and worked in a bank or something, you know, had a sensible job. But I've never been sensible. The only thing I had experience of was army life and leading expeditions. I don't think I could ever do a 9-5 desk job.

**Interviewer:** I guess not! Well, it's been fascinating talking to you. Thank you very much.

**Ralph:** Thank you.

# Speaking Test 2

## Part 2 (Suggested answers)

### Pictures A and B

- **Picture A** shows a "floating" market. The traders are selling their groceries on a special type of boat.
  **Picture B** shows a family shopping at a supermarket. You would find the market in picture A in a country in the Far East, whereas supermarkets can be found all over the Western World.
- It is good to buy groceries from an open market as the goods are often fresher and cheaper than you can find at a supermarket or a grocer's.
- I usually buy my groceries at a small shop down the road, as it means I don't have to carry them very far. Every week there is a large open market in my neighbourhood and I do try to buy vegetables from there as they are very cheap.
- I like to go clothes shopping with my friends as I like to try on all the new fashions. I don't like shopping for shoes as I can never find any I like.

### Pictures C and D

- **Picture C** shows a man painting a picture, whereas **picture D** shows some people riding horses. Painting is quite relaxing, whereas horseriding is very active.
- You only need some paints, a canvas/paper and a paintbrush to paint, but for horseriding you need special clothing, a riding hat and a saddle and bridle for the horse.
- I spend a lot of time playing basketball with my friends. I also watch a lot of television.
- I would like to take up diving as a hobby, as I love swimming and I am fascinated by the things that live underwater.

## Part 3

- **SA:** This could be an advert for a bank or building society.
  **SB:** Yes, they want to give the idea that if you save with them, you will get lots of interest and your money will grow.
- **SA:** The caption might be "Money at the turn of a tap!" since the coins are coming out of a tap like water.
  **SB:** Or another caption could be "Just turn on the tap for your savings."
- **SA:** The picture is eye-catching and makes you think immediately of money.
  **SB:** Yes, there isn't any text to read, so the message is direct.
- **SA:** I think that people with a lot of money to invest might be interested in this.
  **SB:** I think that someone who wants his financial affairs kept simple would appreciate it.

## Part 4

- **SA:** Advertisements can be found almost everywhere; on TV, in newspapers and magazines.
  **SB:** And on billboards, on public transport, in sports stadiums and these days even on food packaging.
- **SA:** People are influenced by advertising in many ways. For example, it can make you want things you don't really need.
  **SB:** It can also make you believe that you will be more successful/attractive if you buy a certain product.
- **SA:** I like the Dixan advert with Roula Koromilla, because she's my favourite TV personality.
  **SB:** I don't like that one, but I like the advertisement for fruit juice where everybody is at the beach having fun.

# Test 3

## Paper 1 - Reading

**Part 1**   1. B      3. C      5. H      7. F
            2. E      4. A      6. D

**Part 2**   8. C (Ln 3-4)      12. B (Ln 18-19)
             9. D (Ln 9)        13. C (Ln 22-23)
            10. A (Ln 10-11)    14. A (Ln 33)
            11. D (Ln 16-17)    15. D (Ln 42)

**Part 3**   16. A   17. G   18. C   19. E   20. B   21. H

**Part 4**   22. B
            23. H
            24. A
            25. F
            26/27. C, G in any order
            28/29. B, F in any order
            30/31. D, E in any order
            32/33. C, H in any order
            34. A
            35. B

## Paper 2 - Writing

### Part 1

Dear Betty,

   I just got your letter telling me about your plans to go to Birden's Health Farm, so I thought I'd better write back straightaway to tell you about my experiences there.

   Birdens say they are offering special discounts, but I have to say that I still found it very expensive. The advert also says that they provide luxurious accommodation, but the rooms are actually very small and uncomfortable. I was very disappointed with my exercise programme, as it appeared that instead of having a personal one designed by the instructor it seemed that there was a standard one for everybody! I also found the meals very small and tasteless, and not delicious as the advert had promised. And the daily massage only lasted five minutes! Before I went I had been looking forward to swimming in their pool, but needless to say I was very disappointed when I found out that the water was stone-cold.

   Overall I must say I was very disappointed with my whole stay at Birden's Health Farm and would urge you to think twice before making your decision.

                          Love,
                          Lisa

### Part 2

3. • Introduce topic
   • Paragraph on benefits of recycling eg. saves paper and thereby forests
   • Paragraph on ways of making it easier eg. move collection points, reduce packaging
   • Conclusion - restate why recycling is important

4. • State purpose of report
   • Describe food - ingredients, occasions eaten etc
   • Describe drink - reasons drunk etc
   • Brief conclusion ie. Greek food eg. "It's tasty and healthy too."

## Paper 3 - Use of English

**Part 1**   1. D    4. A    7. C    10. B    13. A
             2. C    5. B    8. A    11. C    14. C
             3. D    6. D    9. A    12. D    15. B

**Part 2**   16. in                  24. help
            17. with                25. cut
            18. for                 26. next
            19. being               27. could/will/would/
            20. have                    may/might
            21. themselves/life     28. though/however
            22. result              29. many
            23. who                 30. place

**Part 3**   31. ... was nothing he could say ...
            32. ... make/have her phone them ...
            33. ... always make light of ...
            34. ... is an eight-hour flight ...
            35. ... was my grandfather's ...
            36. ... get round to typing ...
            37. ... may be borrowed ...
            38. ... should behave themselves ...
            39. ... are not many people ...
            40. ... only person (who was) not ...

**Part 4**   41. far       46. about      51. too
            42. of        47. out        52. ✓
            43. out       48. a          53. it
            44. ✓         49. ✓          54. the
            45. off       50. ✓          55. ✓

**Part 5**   56. chemistry      61. puzzling
            57. depth(s)       62. evidence
            58. scientists     63. various
            59. mysterious     64. exploration
            60. researchers    65. unsuccessful

## Listening Test 3

**Part 1**    1.  B        3.  B        5.  A        7.  A
              2.  C        4.  C        6.  C        8.  C

**Part 2**    9.   Head Chef
              10.  London College for Chefs
              11.  Food Science (degree)
              12.  22
              13.  trainee chef
              14.  6 months
              15.  broken arm/accident
              16.  cooking fish
              17.  organising people
              18.  creating new/exciting dishes

**Part 3**    19. D    20. A        21. E    22. B    23. C

**Part 4**    24. S        26. G        28. S        30. E
              25. E        27. E        29. G

## Tapescript (Listening Test 3)

### Part 1

*You'll hear people talking in eight different situations. For questions 1 to 8, choose the best answer, A, B or C.*

1. *Listen to this man talking to someone at the check-in desk in Gatwick Airport. Why did he miss his flight to Glasgow?*
   A   He lost his ticket.
   B   Airport officials were on strike.
   C   He was put on the wrong flight in Rome.

   **Man:** Hello, uh... can you help me? I've missed my connecting flight to Glasgow. You see there were delays in Rome.
   **Check-in desk:** Oh yes - the air-traffic controllers' pay dispute. Can I see your ticket please?
   **Man:** Where did I put it... I seem to have lost it... Oh there you go.
   **Check-in desk:** Thank you Mr Gordon. I'll put you on the next flight.
   **Man:** Thanks.

2. *Listen to this conversation between a girl and her mother in a shop. What does Lucy want?*
   A   to try on a long white dress
   B   to have a fairy-tale wedding dress
   C   to wear a fitted, cream dress at her wedding

   **Mother:** Try it on... please Lucy!
   **Lucy:** No! I don't like it.
   **Mother:** But I thought you wanted a frilly white dress.
   **Lucy:** No... *you* want me to have one. I've always said that I want to be married in cream. Something short and slinky - that's what *I* want. Do you really think I want to look like a fairy?

3. *Listen to the conversation between Susan and her friend. Where is Susan going?*
   A   to the dentist for some painkillers
   B   to the pharmacy for some painkillers
   C   to the dentist to have a tooth extracted

   **Friend:** What's the matter Susan?
   **Susan:** It's my tooth - oooh it hurts so much.
   **Friend:** Looks like you need to go to the dentist.
   **Susan:** Oh no!... I can't do that!
   **Friend:** Why not?
   **Susan:** Because he'll insist on pulling it out and it'll hurt even more.
   **Friend:** But doesn't it hurt now?
   **Susan:** Yes! I think I'll just go to the chemist's and get some aspirin.
   **Friend:** Susan, you're such a coward!

4. *Listen to these two friends talking about old family possessions. What did the woman do with her old books?*
   A   throw them away
   B   give them away
   C   sell them

   **Woman:** Well - I wasn't going to put this lot up in the loft - I was all for leaving them out for the dustman. So I boxed them up, ready.
   **Man:** We got a dealer round and got rid of loads of stuff. We made enough to buy a new settee.
   **Woman:** Well this friend of Gary's said he was interested in them. He kept some of them and put some in an auction, along with some other things he'd collected.
   **Man:** Is he on a beach now somewhere in Barbados?
   **Woman:** No - he's a good sort. We're getting a new fridge with our share of the profits.

5. *You hear a man talking on the telephone. Who is he phoning?*
   A   an estate agent
   B   a travel agent
   C   a finance company

   **Man:** We've got two children - so...near to the usual facilities. But not too noisy. (Pause) Well - late summer. (Pause) Well - yes, but hopefully we'll have completed our sale by then. (Pause) Er - three weeks. (Pause) No - not a lot of interest so far, I'm afraid. (Pause) About fifty thousand - but perhaps you can give us an idea of the market. (Pause) No - we've got our own insurance (Pause) Well - the usual interest rates ...

6. *You hear a man asking for advice from a wine merchant. Which wine does the man suggest?*
   A   sweet white wine from France
   B   sweet white wine from Santorini
   C   dry white wine from Greece

**Man:** Hello, can you help me choose a good white wine, please?

**Merchant:** Yes, sir. There are some excellent sweet French and Italian wines, but if you'd like a good, but inexpensive dry white then... try these Greek Santorini wines. This is the one I would choose.

7. *Listen to the shop assistant serving a woman. Which shoes do they have?*

   A   *size 40 in blue, size 39 in black*
   B   *size 40 in blue, size 38 in black*
   C   *size 39 in blue, size 38 in black*

**Woman:** Hello, could I possibly try on this blue shoe in size 39, please?

**Shop assistant:** OK. I'll see if we've got it for you... we have the blue one in a size 40 only. Try it on though because they are really quite a small 40. In size 39 we have only the black in that style. A 38 would definitely be too small I'm afraid.

8. *Listen to this man phoning a workman about a job on his house. Why is he angry?*

   A   *The workman changed the price of the job.*
   B   *The workman didn't work with the builder.*
   C   *The workman left before the job was finished.*

**Man:** But you said the whole thing would be finished in two days. (Pause) But there are still holes around the frames. (Pause) But you said you would work together with a builder - (Pause) No, you didn't say that. (Pause) I don't care - the job isn't finished if there are holes in the wall. I've spoken to the builder - he says he hasn't even been given a day to come and **do** the job. And look how you left the house. (Pause)
Well - that's certainly not what I agreed to pay for.

## Part 2

*You'll hear a woman: being interviewed for a job. For questions 9 to 18, fill in the application form.*

**Interviewer:** Hello, Miss Stevens, please sit down. Now you're here for the job as Head Chef.

**Miss Stevens:** Yes, that's right.

**Interviewer:** Well I have your application form here. I see that you trained at The London College for Chefs.

**Miss Stevens:** Yes that's right, and I studied for a degree in Food Science.

**Interviewer:** Okay, and you graduated when you were 23.

**Miss Stevens:** I was 22. I started training at 23.

**Interviewer:** Ahh, yes I see. (Pause)
It says here you started work as a trainee chef in Coventry. But you only stayed six months. How long was your contract?

**Miss Stevens:** It was for a year actually.

**Interviewer:** So why did you break your contract?

**Miss Stevens:** I had to resign because I broke my arm and it took a long time to heal properly. That's why I had to go.

**Interviewer:** How did you break your arm, if you don't mind me asking?

**Miss Stevens:** No, not at all. I broke it on a fishing trip. I slipped on the boat.

**Interviewer:** Oh dear. So you enjoy fishing?

**Miss Stevens:** I go quite often but really I only do it to catch fresh fish because I enjoy cooking it. It's one of my favourite foods. That's why I particularly want to work in this restaurant.

**Interviewer:** Of course, of course. So what skills do you think you have for this job?

**Miss Stevens:** Well, I'm sure I have all the necessary skills required to run a kitchen in a fine restaurant such as yours. But I suppose if I had to choose something I'm particularly talented in it has to be organising people. I've been told I'm very good at giving clear instructions as to who should do what and how. I would say my other special skill has to be my ability to create new and exciting dishes to please my customers.

**Interviewer:** OK, well thank you for your time. I have another two interviewees to see and then... (fade)

## Part 3

*You'll hear five people talking about beds. For questions 19 to 23, choose from the list of subjects A to F what each speaker is describing. Use the letters only once. There is one extra letter which you do not need to use.*

**Speaker 1 (Male):** When we've got friends or relatives staying we put them in the living room, fold down the settee and leave them there. It's actually very comfortable. You know, you get some of them that are really horrible, with springs sticking in your back, or awkward joins. If my parents are staying over, I'm quite happy to give them my bed while I sleep on it, and I stay up all night watching TV.

**Speaker 2 (Male):** Oh dear, I used to have one of those when I was a child. I positively begged my parents to get one for my bedroom, so that when I had a friend staying the night, you know on a sleep-over, they could stay in my room. However since I've been in the army I can't stand them. If you've got someone above who rolls around a lot in their sleep, you never get any sleep. And if you fall off the top, uh there's a long way to fall!

**Speaker 3 (Female):** Well my husband and I bought it as a bit of a joke really, but since we got it a lot of people have said they're actually good for your back. It's terribly comfortable, it moulds itself to your shape. I feel so relaxed, nothing restrains you, no hard corners. Both of us manage to sleep well although at the beginning I used to get woken up when my husband turned over - I used to feel seasick!.

**Speaker 4 (Female):** It's basically a guest bed. When my sister or one of my friends comes to stay they'll sleep there. It was my bed originally, when I lived on my own, but then when we got married we obviously had to buy a bigger one, because of course it's not really built for two. I couldn't go back to sleeping in a bed like that, I like to stretch out when I'm sleeping.

**Speaker 5 (Male):** My goodness - my parents bought this for me when I was a child. Admittedly, it's not used that often, especially now as we have two small children, but it's strong. It only comes out of the attic every now and again when we have guests. It folds away so it doesn't take up much space. I remember the countless summers sitting by the fire toasting bread, cooking sausages and singing songs. Then we'd all sleep under the stars if the weather was good.

## Part 4

*You'll hear a conversation between three friends who are organising a surprise party for a fourth friend. Answer questions 24 to 30 by writing G (for Gabriel), E (for Evelyn) or S (for Steven) in the boxes provided.*

**Gabriel:** Are we all ready for Saturday then? Evelyn, are you OK? Don't forget you're organising the food - and Steve, you're doing the music.
**Evelyn:** All the food has been planned. I'm picking up the stuff from the supermarket on Saturday.
**Steven:** What are you talking about?
**Evelyn:** It's Basil's birthday.
**Steven:** Not this weekend, is it?
**Evelyn:** I'm afraid it is.
**Steven:** Oh no! I've been so busy with college that...
**Gabriel:** We've all been busy, Steve. And poor Evelyn has even had to sit her Maths and Spanish exams.
**Steven:** I know. And I've got mine on Wednesday. Anyway, you're right, I'd better get a move on if everything needs to be done by the weekend. Is there any chance that either of you might be able to give me a hand?
**Evelyn:** I'm afraid you'll have to count me out. I've already got my hands full.
**Gabriel:** What do you need to do?
**Steven:** Just about everything, Gabriel. I mean, we need to make tapes and...
**Gabriel:** OK. We'll talk about it this evening. I think I can help out with that. Now Evelyn, have all the invites been sent out?
**Evelyn:** Yes, they were sent ages ago. The only person waiting for an invitation was Sam.
**Steven:** Oh, we're not inviting **him**, are we? He ruins everything.
**Evelyn:** I know, but he was given an invitation because he's Basil's friend. In fact I gave it to him in person. Now what about drinks? I think we should order a little more wine, don't you Gab?
**Gabriel:** I think we've got enough already. My dad's bringing some, and as far as I can remember hardly anyone drinks wine.
**Steven:** Yes, it's drinks like cola and juice that we need more of.
**Evelyn:** OK. Steve, I'll see to that. Oh, by the way my sister sent you her best wishes and can't wait to see you at the party. She's sorry about not being able to help out with the preparations, but she'll be here to help clear up.

**Gabriel:** Oh, that's nice of her. It's a shame **my** sister can't make it. She's on duty at the weekend. She tried to get the time off, but she couldn't.
**Steven:** Never mind, Gab. We'll be videoing Basil's face when he walks into the house and sees us all there!!... Anyway if we've finished for tonight, I'm off. I've got to get to the coach station before it closes. I need to meet a friend who's bought me some tickets.
**Evelyn:** Oh, you couldn't do me a favour and drop me off at the train station? I've arranged to see Angela there at 8pm.
**Steven:** Sure.

## Speaking Test 3

### Part 2 (Suggested answers)

#### Pictures A and B

- **Picture A** shows some soldiers who are fighting in a war, or doing some military training. There are also some helicopters hovering overhead. **Picture B** shows a person holding a white dove in their hands.
- Picture A represents war, and picture B peace.
- In many cases I think war can be prevented if people would just sit down and talk about their differences and problems. However, most people do not think rationally when they are planning a war and so it cannot be prevented.
- I think military service is important as it teaches everybody how to fight in case of a war. However I think women should also be given the chance to do military service so that they too can learn skills that would be useful during a war.

#### Pictures C and D

- **Picture C** shows some plants growing in the middle of the earth. Picture **D** shows a model of the earth being sprayed with something like hairspray. Picture D shows how the world is being destroyed whereas picture C is about caring for the earth.
- Our environment is at risk from pollution, which is damaging the ozone layer. Factories and cars produce a lot of poisonous gases which are poisoning the atmosphere and causing acid rain. Also the rainforests are being destroyed, which is causing worldwide environmental problems.
- I feel very strongly about environmental issues. It is very important that every individual does something now to try and help save the environment before it is too late.
- People can use electric cars instead of cars that use petrol. We can recycle our rubbish such as bottles, cans and paper, and leftover food can be used to make compost for the garden. We can also make sure we don't buy products whose production or use damages the environment.

## Part 3

- **SA:** Well, all the pictures seem to have something to do with outer space.
  **SB:** Yes, the first picture shows a space station. In the future people may be able to live on space stations like these.
- **SA:** Whereas the second picture looks as though it's showing an alien: a type of being that you could find on another planet if you went there.
  **SB:** It might even be able to visit us on earth. There are always reports of people claiming to have met aliens.
  **SB:** The third picture shows a flying saucer or UFO. A lot of people say they have seen something like this flying through our skies.
- **SA:** Some people even think they have travelled on one.
- **SA:** The last picture could be showing what another planet looks like. The sea seems to be floating above the land and there are various planets which are resting very close to the surface. It looks very cold.
  **SB:** So it seems that science fiction is the link between all the pictures, as they all show things that either do not yet exist (in the case of the space station) or have not been proven to exist.
- **SA:** Or at least - not yet!

## Part 4

- **SA:** I think that there must be life on other planets. Why would there only be life on ours?
  **SB:** I disagree. I think all the other planets in our solar system are unable to support any life form.
- **SA:** I think it is possible that UFOs carrying aliens do exist, but in no form that we can ever imagine.
  **SB:** I disagree. I think any sightings of UFOs have natural explanations.
- **SA:** I think that it is very possible that humans will live on other planets in the future, although in a very controlled environment.
  **SB:** I agree. NASA and scientists are already very close to making it possible for people to live in space, so living on another planet is just the next step.

# Test 4

## Paper 1 - Reading

**Part 1**   1. A   2. G   3. C   4. H   5. B   6. F

**Part 2**
- 7.  C (Ln 5-6)
- 8.  D (Ln 2-5)
- 9.  A (Ln 7-13)
- 10. A (Ln 13-15)
- 11. D (Ln 21-22)
- 12. A (Ln 29-30)
- 13. B (Ln 33-35)

**Part 3**
- 14. H
- 15. A
- 16. I
- 17. F
- 18. B
- 19. G
- 20. E

**Part 4**
- 21/22. A, D in any order
- 23/24. B, D in any order
- 25. D
- 26. E
- 27/28. C, E in any order
- 29/30. B, D in any order
- 31/32/33. A, C, D in any order
- 34. B
- 35. A

## Paper 2 - Writing

**Part 1**

Dear Mr Ware,

I am writing to you regarding the conference that is planned for Sunday July 23rd.

I must apologise for the fact that I will no longer be able to collect you from the airport as I had at first hoped. Unfortunately, I have to attend a christening half an hour earlier at a church some distance from the airport.

It would be easiest if you catch a taxi straight from the airport to the Dun Cow Hotel, where the conference is being held. The conference does not start until 12 noon and so you should have time to freshen up before the talk. Lunch is at 2pm followed by an open discussion where people will be able to ask questions.

I wish to apologise again for this change of plan, and I hope that it does not inconvenience you in any way.

Yours sincerely,
John Bidden

## Part 2

**3.** • Introduction - Delphi
 • Paragraph on different sights: oracle, Apollo's temple, stadium, museum
 • Paragraph about nearby villages/towns, suggested places to eat/stay
 • Conclusion: well worth a visit because it is of great historical and archaeological interest and set in breathtaking surroundings. Plenty of places to eat and opportunities to buy local crafts.

**4.** • State purpose of report
 • State positive points eg certain facilities are very good and well-maintained, impressed by children's playgrounds etc
 • State negative points eg parks were dirty and seemed neglected, flowerbeds not well cared for, gardening staff unenthusiastic
 • Conclusion: sum up and make suggestions eg more investment in parks, further training for staff.

## Paper 3 - Use of English

**Part 1**
| | | | | |
|---|---|---|---|---|
| 1. A | 4. D | 7. B | 10. B | 13. C |
| 2. D | 5. B | 8. C | 11. A | 14. D |
| 3. C | 6. A | 9. C | 12. D | 15. A |

**Part 2**
| | | | |
|---|---|---|---|
| 16. up | | 24. although |
| 17. than | | 25. make |
| 18. be | | 26. while |
| 19. of | | 27. between/in |
| 20. which/that | | 28. example |
| 21. are | | 29. have/feel |
| 22. tongue | | 30. where |
| 23. own | | |

**Part 3**
31. ... only country she has not ...
32. ... for fear of being ...
33. ... had no opportunity to thank ...
34. ... accused Dick of breaking her ...
35. ... had/got my leg bitten by/was bitten on the leg ...
36. ... to turn up for/at ...
37. ... wishes she had gone to ...
38. ... for having a map ...
39. ... the nail on the head ...
40. ... too spicy for me to ...

**Part 4**
| | | | | |
|---|---|---|---|---|
| 41. the | 45. ✓ | 49. ✓ | 53. from |
| 42. that | 46. been | 50. with | 54. to |
| 43. ✓ | 47. it | 51. had | 55. for |
| 44. the | 48. ✓ | 52. ✓ | |

**Part 5**
| | |
|---|---|
| 56. popularity | 61. suitable |
| 57. relaxation | 62. imagination |
| 58. enjoyable | 63. sympathetic |
| 59. passively | 64. depths |
| 60. producers | 65. dissatisfaction |

## Listening Test 4

**Part 1**
| | | | |
|---|---|---|---|
| 1. B | 3. C | 5. A | 7. B |
| 2. B | 4. B | 6. C | 8. B |

**Part 2**
9. 30 - 39
10. sports teacher
11. no
12. (nearly) four years
13. dissatisfied
14. two
15. one
16. local newspaper
17. sports magazine
18. £400

**Part 3**   19. F   20. D   21. A   22. E   23. B

**Part 4**
| | | | |
|---|---|---|---|
| 24. M | 26. J | 28. M | 30. M |
| 25. C | 27. C | 29. J | |

### Tapescript (Listening Test 4)

#### Part 1

*You'll hear people talking in eight different situations. For questions 1 to 8, choose the best answer A, B or C.*

**1.** *You will hear a man talking about his work. What does he do?*
 *A He makes clothes.*
 *B He makes lamps.*
 *C He makes furniture.*

**Man:** I make them to order. Customers tell me what they want and I produce them. They give me the size they want, the colour, the material for the base, the style of shade and so on. I draw them a design and if they like it, I start working. I'm very busy because people like my stuff and, after all, everybody needs some light in their lives.

**2.** *Listen to this person talking about Chris Livingstone. Who is he?*
 *A an army general*
 *B a reporter*
 *C a politician*

**Host:** I am pleased and honoured to introduce our guest this evening. Over the past months he has brought home to us the tragedy and devastation in the former Soviet Union. He has caused headaches for many an army general - refusing to be silenced as the battles rage. In his impartial quest for the truth he has challenged politician after politician, demanding answers and settling for nothing but the truth. First on the scene wherever it matters and here with us tonight. Ladies and gentlemen - a warm welcome please for Chris Livingstone.

3.  *You overhear this man talking. Why is he going to be late?*
    A   *He's going to his mother's.*
    B   *He's going to the dentist.*
    C   *He's going to his brother's.*

    **Man:** I'll definitely be there, but I might be a bit late. I've got to go round to my brother's quickly to let him know about mum. She's not been very well so I thought I should tell him, and he hasn't got a tele- phone you know. I have to telephone the dentist on the way there as well because I'll have to cancel my appointment.

4.  *You are at a friend's house and you hear this conversa-tion. Where has Gareth gone?*
    A   *to bed*
    B   *out*
    C   *home*

    **Man:** Gareth's gone without drinking his coffee. Shall I pour it away?
    **Woman:** Might as well - it'll be stone cold when he gets back.
    **Man:** Has Elizabeth gone home? She was looking like she needed to go to bed more than Gareth.
    **Woman:** I know. He's just running her back home. Put the kettle on and I'll make him another drink.

5.  *You overhear these two friends talking. What has the young man decided to do?*
    A   *to take the job*
    B   *not to take the job*
    C   *he doesn't know yet*

    **Man 1:** Are you going to go for that garage job?
    **Man 2:** Well, they said they'd have me - it's a bit beyond me though. Still - if I don't give it  a try I'll  n e v e r know, will I?
    **Man 1:** Suppose you make a mess of things?
    **Man 2:** Then I'll get the sack!
    **Man 1:** Well - that wouldn't look too good on your C.V. would it?
    **Man 2:** Never mind - I don't know how much that matters anyway.

6.  *You overhear this in a TV studio. Why does the director want to film again?*
    A   *The sound was too low.*
    B   *The cameras were too close.*
    C   *The acting was bad.*

    **Director:** Cut, cut! We'll have to do that again I'm afraid. Camera one and two, can you stay where you are?  Tony, I need something more. You're supposed

to be at a funeral, so show some **emotion**. Sound, you were just a touch too close - could you pull back a bit please?

7.  *You hear this man telling a friend about his bank. Who or what made a mistake?*
    A   *the cashpoint*
    B   *the man himself*
    C   *the bank cashier*

    **Man:** Well - I went to the bank and put in £125 and that should have made my balance £295. The cashier brought my book up to date. Then I left, and a while later I wanted some money so I drew £20 out of a cashpoint. It gave me a receipt which said my total was now £215. I just couldn't work out where £60 had gone in half an hour. At home my wife told me I had taken out £60 the week before. I just forgot about that extra bit I took out to pay the rent.

8.  *You hear a firefighter talking about the probable cause of a fire. How does he think the fire started?*
    A   *It was started deliberately.*
    B   *There was a problem with the electricity.*
    C   *There was an electrical storm.*

    **Fire Officer:** Well, we can't rule out the possibility that the fire was deliberately started. There's a strong smell of petrol in the air, but that probably comes from the garage. It looks more likely that it was an electrical fault. I think that this plug is the culprit. Someone may have left a cigarette burning, but I doubt it.

## Part 2

*You'll hear a man in the street being interviewed for a radio programme. For questions 9 to 18, complete the questionnaire.*

**Interviewer:** Hello. I wonder if you could spare a few moments of your time to answer a few questions for a survey. It's being conducted by Radio West.
**Interviewee:** Certainly. Does that mean my com-ments will be broadcast on the radio?
**Interviewer:** Not necessarily. We only have ten mi-nutes of air time and we want to include as many comments as possible. Now, can you just tell me which age group you belong to. Is it the 20-29 age group or the 30-39?
**Interviewee:** I was in the 20-29 age group, until last week, that is!
**Interviewer:** And your occupation?
**Interviewee:** I'm a sports teacher.
**Interviewer:** Oh, how suitable. Our survey is on the town's sports facilities.
**Interviewee:** Really?
**Interviewer:** So you're not self-employed?
**Interviewee:** That's right.
**Interviewer:** How long have you been in your present job?
**Interviewee:** Ooh! Let me think now...at least three years, it must be...yes, nearly four years.

*Interviewer:* Are you satisfied with the town's sports facilities?

*Interviewee:* Well, I'm glad somebody has bothered to look into this. My students have a terrible time trying to book tennis courts and organising football matches during the holidays. So for my students' sake I have to say I'm not.

*Interviewer:* Can I just ask you if you know how many tennis courts there are in the town?

*Interviewee:* Well, I know of two. And they are always overbooked.

*Interviewer:* That's interesting. And how many swimming pools are there in the town...that you know of, I mean?

*Interviewee:* Just the one. The big public one near the common.

*Interviewer:* Very interesting. The council wanted this survey conducted and broadcast on Radio West. They were concerned that people didn't know about the town's facilities. And they seem to be right. The problem is not the lack of places to go. It's the lack of advertising.

*Interviewee:* Why, how many tennis courts are there?

*Interviewer:* There are eight tennis courts and four public swimming pools. Where do you yourself look for sports notices?

*Interviewee:* Er, the local newspaper usually.

*Interviewer:* Anywhere else?

*Interviewee:* A sports magazine.

*Interviewer:* And finally sir, can I just ask you how much you spend on sport per year?

*Interviewee:* Well, let me think...er...approximately three, no, more like four hundred pounds, and that includes all the equipment and membership fees.

*Interviewer:* Well, thank you very much for your time, sir.

**Interviewee:** Thank you.

## Part 3

*You'll hear five people talking about their favourite drinks. For questions 19 to 23, choose from the list A to F the drink each speaker prefers. There is one extra letter which you do not need to use. Use the letters only once.*

*Speaker 1 (Female):* I was so worried when my kids were growing up that their teeth would decay if they drank too much. I would only let them have a bit once a week. I think it's very sweet and sickly but I enjoy a glass every now and then. It's that sparkling sensation in your mouth that's nice. It's great with ice on a hot summer's day. The kids like the lemon taste best, and I treat them to one whenever we go to a fast food place after we've been shopping.

*Speaker 2 (Male):* This is a very old traditional drink. My father used to tell me stories of his father who made it, but it's quite a difficult drink to make. It takes good ingredients and time. It's an international drink too. The Dutch and Germans are supposed to be good at making it, but I prefer the English myself! You

can buy it in bottles, or even cans these days. Most people like to drink it with friends or with a meal. Of course wine-lovers consider it a baby's drink, but I wouldn't agree with that at all.

*Speaker 3 (Male):* I drink this a lot now. It's such a versatile drink. I love it blended with bananas or strawberries. Some people say it's not really a drink but a nutritious meal. Sometimes I have it warm with honey, because it makes me sleep better. I like the adverts for it in the magazines and on television. They say not only kids, but adults need it too. They say you should drink it semi-skimmed.

*Speaker 4 (Female):* My husband drinks nothing else, ever since we came back from our holiday in the Caribbean. It was so cheap out there. Every drink they offered you was fresh and natural and we were spoiled for choice. You just had to look at the trees and you understood why. We really liked the cocktails too and when they poured them in the glass they were all different colours, even milky white. I never buy them in cartons from the shop. They seem to have more sugar and I think they're bad for you.

*Speaker 5 (Female):* Most countries make and bottle their own. Usually different kinds are made in different regions. I love to drink a glass with my meal or when I go out in the evening. My husband likes a glass too. We've started buying cartons of it, but that's a fairly new idea. Last week we went on a picnic and we found that they came in very handy - no corkscrew was needed. It's the drink of the gods so they say. Well, I can never make up my mind whether I prefer the fruity sparkling kind or the rich and dry kind. It depends on what you eat I suppose. I like it to be dry if we're eating chicken. I'd like to have a go at making my own sometime.

## Part 4

*You'll hear a conversation that takes place between a couple and a check-in clerk at the airport. Answer questions 24 to 30 by writing M (for Mary Huckles), J (for James Huckles), or C (for check-in clerk) in the boxes provided.*

*Check-in Clerk:* Can I have your tickets please?

*James Huckles:* (breathless) Er...here you are. We're booked on the 6 o'clock flight to Malaga. We're not too late, are we?

*Check-in Clerk:* Let me see. I think you've got a couple of minutes to get to the departure gate.

*Mary Huckles:* (angry) A couple of minutes!! Oh, James we're always doing things in a hurry. I hate being late! I wanted to do some duty free shopping.

*James Huckles:* It's OK, darling. We can get some presents when we arrive.

*Mary Huckles:* But that's not the same!

*Check-in Clerk:* It's still possible for you to buy something on the flight. I realise the selection might be somewhat limited, but there are still some good bargains available.

*Mary Huckles:* Oh, I suppose that'll have to do.
*Check-in Clerk:* Now is this all the luggage you have?
*James Huckles:* Er, yes.
*Check-in Clerk:* OK. Thank you, here are your tickets. If you head for Gate 8 somebody will still be there to take you to the aeroplane.
*James Huckles:* What about this bag?
*Check-in Clerk:* Oh, goodness. I must have missed it in the rush to check you onto the flight.
*James Huckles:* Now Mary, there's no need to hurry. We'll get there on time.
*Check-in Clerk:* I'm afraid you'll have to get a move on, though. Even though you've checked in, there's no guarantee the captain will wait more than a few minutes for passengers who are late. Oh, by the way, I have to ask you for security reasons if you have any electrical appliances in your bag?
*Mary Huckles:* Nothing as far as I can remember. Oh! A hairdryer. Oh, but no, I think I left it at home in the rush.
*Check-in Clerk:* Well, I can see something on the screen here. It's showing me what looks like a ...
*Mary Huckles:* Nonsense. There's nothing electrical.
*James Huckles:* No darling, she's right. I put the hairdryer in at the last minute just in case we needed it. It's in that one over there.
*Check-in Clerk:* That's right sir. Now if you'd just like to make your way to Gate 8 ...
*James Huckles:* Can somebody help us with our hand luggage?
*Check-in Clerk:* Er...I'm afraid there's no one around at the moment. Ah, hold on there's a porter. Oh, no it's a cleaner.
*James Huckles:* Oh. I see one. Porter! Here he comes.
*Check-in Clerk:* Now do have a wonderful time out in Malaga.
*Mary Huckles:* (anxious) Thank you. I just hope we get on the plane. I mean, it could still leave without us...

# Speaking Test 4

## Part 2 (Suggested answers)

### Pictures A and B

- **Picture A** shows a road full of people on bicycles, whereas **picture B** shows a number of cars driving along a motorway.
- Bicycles are a good means of transport as they don't produce any pollution, and they are also a good way of keeping fit. However cars are better for travelling long distances as they are faster and more comfortable.
- I would choose to travel by bicycle in the city as it's easy to get from place to place and you don't get stuck in traffic jams. Cars are better for the countryside as the distances between the places are greater, and you may want to get there quickly.

- I think people will travel with electric cars in the future. Many people may have their own small private aeroplanes for travelling between cities.

### Pictures C and D

- **Picture C** shows a crowded city centre, I think it's in Tokyo. **Picture D** shows some mud huts which are possibly in a village in Africa.
- I would prefer to live in the city because, even though there are a lot of people and it's noisy, at least you can live comfortably. I think life in an African village would be very difficult, as there would be no electricity, running water or other amenities.
- Development can bring prosperity to a place, and can bring an end to diseases with proper drainage and housing.
- Development can destroy a lot of native culture, which is something that is happening all over the world as places are overwhelmed by western culture. Communities are often not very close in cities, and so there are a lot of lonely people there.

## Part 3

- **SA:** People need to be made aware that disabled people are no different to anyone else and so should not be treated any differently.
  **SB:** We could also make it easier for disabled people to get around - at the moment many places are inaccessible if you are in a wheelchair. There should be ramps outside all buildings, and pavements should be fixed so that people in wheelchairs can pass along them easily and cross roads.
- **SA:** Measures should be taken so that disabled people can take public transport as well.

## Part 4

- **SA:** There don't seem to be any facilities for the disabled where I live.
  **SB:** That's probably why you see very few disabled people out and about.
- **SA:** Disabled people are looked after by their relatives.
  **SB:** They are also looked after in special homes, and there are people who are trained to care for them properly.
- **SA:** The government should make sure that disabled people are able to pass along all pavements.
  **SB:** Public buildings should have proper access for wheelchairs.
- **SA:** Public schools should be able to take disabled children so that any children with problems are integrated into society at an early age.
  **SB:** Yes, and public toilets should also have toilets for the disabled.

# Supplementary Reading Comprehension material

## Breakneck Boys

| | |
|---|---|
| 1. B | 5. D | 8. B | 11. B | 14. D |
| 2. A | 6. C | 9. D | 12. C | 15. C |
| 3,4. B, C (in any order) | 7. C | 10. C | 13. B | |

## Worldwide Japanese Cooking

| | |
|---|---|
| 1,2. A, C (in any order) | 5. A | 8. E | 11. A | 14. C |
| 3. A | 6. B | 9. C | 12. B | 15. C |
| 4. E | 7. C | 10. D | 13. A | |

## Mothers and Childcare

| | | | | |
|---|---|---|---|---|
| 1. D | 4. C | 7. B | 10. B | 13. D |
| 2. A | 5. E | 8. A | 11. B | 14. C |
| 3. C | 6. E | 9. D | 12. E | 15. E |